Praise for RUMI

"Rumi's *rubaiyat* were almost certainly thrown off extempore and recorded by his disciples; in these clear, accurate, vivid, and often very beautiful versions we come as close as is possible in English to catching the evanescent moment of composition, the thought as it flickers from Rumi's mind out into the world."
–Richard Davis, Professor Emeritus, Ohio State University; translator of *The Conference of the Birds*, *Shahnameh*, and *Vis and Ramin*

"What could be more exciting than to have the vast erudition of Amin Banani and the spiritual sensibility of Anthony A. Lee applied to bringing Rumi's poetry into English? A tour de force that no one interested in the work of the great Persian Sufi master can afford to miss!"
–Juan Cole, Professor of Middle East History, University of Michigan; prominent blogger and essayist

"Anthony A. Lee, a brilliant poet in his own right, has brought rarely-translated Rumi quatrains into English. Dazzling poems, sparkling word choice, fair order: a true idea on each page informs & brings light to me, to you, to every reader."
–Catherine Daly, poet, teacher; author of six poetry collections, including *Vauxhall*, *Locket*, and *Da Da Da*

"These poems are rendered with such finesse and passion, a unique combination that captures that same unique combination we find in Rumi, who touches our hearts as well as our mind and spirit. Lee's translations find that perfect balance and give us Rumi as if he were sitting in front of us, speaking."
—Jack Grapes, poet, teacher, publisher

"The volume here features a collaboration between a master of Persian poetry and a distinguished American poet. These collaborations may well be the necessary model needed to come up with translations that are both faithful to the original and beautiful in the new language. Rumi lovers will no doubt appreciate this new collaboration."
—Omid Safi is a Professor of Islamic Studies at the University of North Carolina at Chapel Hill and author of *Memories of Muhammad*

RUMI

53 Secrets from the Tavern of Love

RUMI

53 Secrets from the Tavern of Love

Poems from the *Rubaiyat* of Mowlana Rumi

translated by
Amin Banani & Anthony A. Lee

White Cloud Press
Ashland, Oregon

Kalimat Press
Los Angeles

White Cloud Press books may be purchased for educational, business, or sales promotional use. For information, please write: Special Market Department, White Cloud Press, PO Box 3400, Ashland, OR 97520
Website: www.whitecloudpress.com

Published in association with: Kalimat Press, 1600 Sawetelle Boulevard, Suite 310, Los Angeles, CA 90025
Website: www.kalimat.com

Cover image copyright © The Metropolitan Museum of Art
Cover and Interior Design by C Book Services

First edition, 2014
Printed in the United States of America

19 18 17 16 15 14   5 4 3 2 1

Library of Congress Cataloging-in-Publication Data

Jalal al-Din Rumi, Maulana, 1207-1273.
[Poems. Selections. English]
 RUMI - 53 secrets from the tavern of love : poems from the Rubiayat of Mevlana Rumi / translated by Amin Banani ; translated by Anthony A. Lee.
   pages cm. — (Islamic Encounter series)
  ISBN 978-1-940468-00-6 (paperback)
 1. Jalal al-Din Rumi, Maulana, 1207-1273—Translations into English. 2. Sufi poetry, Persian—Translations into English. I. Banani, Amin, 1926-2013, translator. II. Lee, Anthony A., 1947- translator. III. Title.
 PK6480.E5B34 2014
 891'.5511—dc23

                              2014003055

Table of Contents

Translating Rumi

Anthony A. Lee

On Saturday, November 29, 1244 C.E. by our calendar, in the city of Konya in medieval Anatolia (now, southern Turkey), an event took place that would change the course of Islamic history, and eventually change the consciousness of humanity. Mowlana Jalal al-Din Muhammad, known to us as Rumi, a Muslim cleric and legal scholar, fell in love. This was a strange and sudden, burning, ecstatic love that opened his heart and introduced new worlds to him. Even today, Sufi devotees around the world celebrate the legacy of that day in music and dance and poetry.

The focus of Rumi's love was Shams-e Tabrizi (literally, the Sun of Tabriz), a wanderer and fellow Muslim scholar. Legend tells us that it was almost love at first sight. In the marketplace of Konya, amid the cotton stalls, sugar vendors, and vegetable stands, Rumi rode through the street, surrounded by his students. Shams caught hold of the reins of his donkey and rudely challenged the master with two questions. "Who was the greater mystic, Bayazid (a Sufi saint) or Muhammad?" Shams demanded.

"What a strange question! Muhammad is greater than all the saints," Rumi replied.

"So, why is it then that Muhammad said to God, 'I didn't know you as I should have,' while Bayazid proclaimed, 'Glory be to me! How exalted is my Glory!'? (That is, he claimed the station of God himself.)"

Rumi explained that Muhammad was the greater of the two, because Bayazid could be filled to capacity by a single experience of divine blessings. He lost himself completely and was filled with God. Muhammad's capacity was unlimited and could never be filled. His desire was endless, and he was always thirsty. With every moment he came closer to God, and then regretted his former distant state. For that reason, he said, "I have never known you as I should have."

It is recorded that after this exchange of words, Rumi felt a window open at the top of his head and saw smoke rise to heaven. He cried out, fell to the ground, and lost consciousness for one hour. Shams, upon hearing these answers, realized that he was face-to-face with the object of his longing, the one he had prayed for God to send him. When Rumi awoke, he took Shams's hand, and the two of them returned to Rumi's school together on foot. They secluded themselves for forty days, speaking to no others.

Rumi and Shams of Tabriz

Rumi was born in the year 1207, at the eastern edge of the Persian-speaking, Islamic world near the city of Balkh in what is now Afghanistan, then part of the Persian empire. He was named Muhammad Jalal al-Din, though he is known to us in the West as Rumi (after Rom, the area of Anatolia where he eventually made his home). Throughout the East, however, he is known universally and exclusively as Mowlana (the Master). His father, Baha al-Din Valad, was a Muslim cleric, a theologian, and a mystic teacher. The son followed his father, and Rumi received a full, traditional Islamic education, studying with Baha al-Din and with several prominent religious scholars, finally becoming a teacher in his own right.

While Rumi was still a boy, his family moved from Balkh, some years ahead of the Mongol invasions that would eventually devastate the city in 1221. Baha al-Din probably found it necessary to relocate because he was under attack by conservative and legalistic Muslim clerics who objected to his mystical ideas. For a decade, the family wandered from city to city. They traveled to Iran, to Baghdad, to Armenia, and made the pilgrimage to Mecca. During this period, at the age of seventeen, Rumi married Gowhar Khatun, the daughter of two of his father's disciples. He eventually had two sons with her. When she died some years later (1243?), Rumi married a widow, Kerra Khatun, with whom he had two children, a son and a daughter.

After Rumi's first marriage, his father, Baha al-Din, was invited by the Sultan of Konya to move to Anatolia and live there. The sultan built a college (*madrasa*) for the father in Konya where he taught for two years before his death in 1231, when Rumi was twenty-four years old. The son would eventually, after completing his studies, assume the mantle of his father and teach as the master of that same college.

Despite his very prominent position in Konya, Rumi's mystical yearnings remained unfulfilled. When he met the wild, wandering scholar, Shams-e Tabrizi, he was transformed. As Rumi describes the initial encounter: he felt as though he was raw, and then cooked, and then consumed completely, turned to ash. Shams was, of course, a native of Tabriz, in Iran. A fully educated scholar, he had left his native city as a very young man in search of knowledge and spiritual realization. He studied under many masters, but always quarreled with them. He searched from city to city, but found no one with whom he could share his own profound spiritual insights. Finally, he prayed to God to allow him to find a true friend. In a dream, his answer was: "He is in Anatolia."

The adoring friendship which resulted between Rumi and Shams was instant and reciprocal. Each saw in the other the face of God, a reflection of self and of ultimate reality. Rumi attached himself to Shams as a student and disciple. Almost all of Rumi's poems sing of his passion for Shams and what he represented. Rumi named his collected body of poems the *Divan-e Shams-e Tabrizi*, meaning, the collected poems of (or for; or by) Shams of Tabriz. Immediately after his first meeting with Shams, Rumi abandoned his students, broke off his teaching, ceased his preaching in the college and mosque, and spent all of his time with Shams, receiving his instruction and sharing with him Sufi mystic exercises of music, prayer, movement, and dance.

Many in Konya, and especially Rumi's neglected students, became increasingly jealous of Shams and hostile towards his influence over their master. Tensions became so serious that, after two years in Konya, Shams departed from the city without warning, leaving no word of his whereabouts. Rumi was desolate, paralyzed by grief, and he fell sick. He sent his son in search of Shams, and when he was discovered in Damascus, Shams returned. But shortly after that, he departed once more and was never seen again. Legend suggests that Shams was actually murdered by Rumi's disciples who were desperate to destroy his influence over their master and continue their education.[1]

For years after, Rumi grieved and hoped that he would find Shams still alive. He was inconsolable. Twice, Rumi traveled to Damascus himself in search of Shams. But he never found him. In his uncontrollable bereavement, he was transformed from an intellectual into a poet. It was during this period that a volcano of mystic poems erupted from his lips, with its white-hot flow. The number of Rumi's poems is truly remarkable. There are thousands of lyric poems (*ghazals*) that survive in his collection. Of the shorter poems of the kind translated in this volume, the quatrains (*rubaiyat*), one Persian edition has collected 1,994 of them.

---

1. Current scholarship holds that the legend of Shams's death at the hands of Rumi's disciples is unlikely. For a discussion of the issues, see Franklin D. Lewis, *Rumi: Past and Present, East and West* (Oxford: Oneworld, 2000), pp. 197-200.

Truth

In your wild dreams, what are you looking for?
In tears and blood, what are you looking for?
You—from head to foot—you are the Truth.
You can't find yourself! What are you looking for?

یک چند به تقلید گزیدیم خود را
نادیده، به هستی نام شنیدیم خود را

در خود بودم، زان نَسزیدیم خود را
از خود چو برون شدم، بدیدیم خود را

Labyrinth

Like all the rest, I was full of myself.
Blind, I just wanted a name for myself.
I locked my soul in the prison of self.
When I escaped from there, I found myself.

شمعیست دل مرد پر او فروختنی
چاکیست زهجر دوست بردوختنی

ای بی خبر از ساختن و سوختنی
عشق آمدنی بود نه آموختنی

Love

The candle inside your heart: Let it burn!
That gap keeps you from the Friend: Let it turn!
Hey! Don't you know about pain and burning?
Love comes like that. It's not something you learn.

گر در طلب منزل جانی، جانی
گر در طلب لقمهٔ نانی، نانی

این نکتهٔ رمز اگر بدانی، دانی
هر چیز که در جستن آنی، آنی

You Are That

You're looking for soul—but you are the soul.
You're searching for crumbs—you are loaf and roll.
Learn this secret, then you'll know: Whatever
you're seeking—you are that. You are the goal.

آن شمع رخ تو گلگئی مینت بیا
وان نقش تو از آب منی نیست بیا

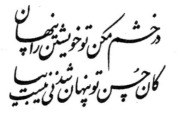

در خشم مکن تو خویشتن را پنهان
کان حسن تو پنهان شدنی نیست بیا

Come Here

That light wasn't in your mom's womb. Come here.
That face didn't jump from your father's loin.
Come here. Don't destroy yourself with anger,
because you can't hide your beauty. Come here.

از شبنم عشق خاک آدم گل شد
صد فتنه و شور در جهان حاصل شد

صد نشتر عشق بر رگ روح زدند
یک قطره از آن چکید و نامش دل شد

The Spill

He shaped Adam from specks of love and dust—
then came a world of treachery and lust.
They made a hundred cuts to kill his soul.
But one drop spilled—that one became his heart.

تا پردهٔ اندیشه گری را ندری
تو پرده در اسپی، پرده دری پرده وری

گویی تو که: من ز هر هنر باخبرم
این بی‌خبری بس که ز خود بی‌خبری

Veil of Reason

This veil of reason, you must rip it down!
It's just a curtain you are peeking 'round.
"I have studied every science," you say?
It's knowledge of yourself you haven't found.

از آب حیات دوست بیمار نما

در گلبن وصل دوست گلخار نما

گویند دریچه‌ای‌ست از دل سوی دل

چه جای دریچه‌ای که دیوار نما

Rose Garden

Find the water of life, drink, and be healed.
Find the Friend in the rose garden—no thorns.
They say there's a window from heart to heart.
But, why a window?—there are no walls here.

با هستی و نیستیم یگانگیست
وز هر دو بریدیم، نه فرّانگیست

گر من ز عجایبی که در دل دارم
دیوانه نمی‌شوم، ز دیوانگیست

Being

To be or not to be—well, I don't care.

Forget them both! There is no honor there.

If I'm not mad by now, then that's madness.

My heart is filled with joy, so I don't care.

در میکده عشق حق چنین مست کدید
خمها همه در شکسته و بست کدید

صحن زمی و سقف فلک را پری
همچون قدحی گرفته در دست کدید

The Tavern of Love

In the tavern of love, what drunks you see!
The casks are smashed and overturned. You see!
Wine is on the floor. Wine rains from the sky!
But no one has his cup in hand, you see.

ای دل همه رخت را در این کوی انداز
پیراهن یوسف است بر روی انداز

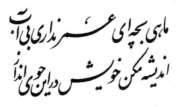

ماهی بچه‌ای عمر نداری بی آب
اندیشه مکن خویش در این جوی انداز

Don't Think

Go throw your clothes in the street. Be clean!
Cover your shame with Joseph's shirt, and dream!
A little fish can't live without water.
Don't think! Throw yourself naked in this stream.

ما پیش از چار ده می بینیم
بی چشم و بی چشم و بوی ماه رو می بینیم

گفتی که : از و همه جهان آب شدست
آوخ ! که در این آب چه مه می بینیم

Half Moon

The moon's half dark—to me it's bright and full.
With eyes closed shut, still I can feel it full.
Once you said: He has melted down the world!
Look! In the water, I see the moon full.

گر بوی نمی‌بری درین کوی میا
ور جامه نمی‌کنی درین جوی میا

آنسوی که سوی‌ها از آنسوی آمد
می‌باش هم‌آنسوی و بدین سوی میا

Don't Come Here

If you can't smell flowers in this alley—
don't come here! . . . Can't get naked in this stream?
Don't swim here! That place with four directions
back there: That's your side. Stay there! Don't come here!

عاشق تو پُری شوی بر و پَشم بریس
صد کاری و صد رنگی و صد پیشه ورپیس

درکاسهٔ سر چو نیست باده عشق
در مطبخِ مدخلان برو کاسه بلیس

If You're Not in Love

If you're not in love, go spin wool instead.
Go on! Do anything you like. Instead,
in the kitchen, lick the cups of lovers—
since there's no wine of love inside your head.

ای حیف، که پیش گزنی طنبوری
یا یوسف، همخانه شود با کوری

یاقوت نهی، در دهن رنجوری
یا جفت شود محنثی با حوری

Such a Waste!

Such a waste! To play music for the deaf,
or for a blind man to live with Joseph—
sugar cubes for the sick—an impotent
man trying to make love to a virgin.

با صورت دین صورت زردشت کشتی
چون خسر، نخوری نبات و بر پشت کشتی

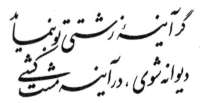

گر آینهٔ زردشتی تو نما
دیوانه شوی، در آینه مشت کشتی

Religion

You wear religion's mask, then paint idols.
You ass! You carry sweets, but can't eat them.
If you could see your ugly face in the
mirror—you'd go mad and break the mirror.

شب گشت و ندانیت خبر از شب و از روز
روزاست شبم، ز روی آن نوراَفروز

ای شب، شب از آنی که از او بی خبری
ای روز، برو، ز روز او، روز آموز

36

It's Dark

It's dark, yet the light of his face will shine.

Midday is night, unless his face will shine.

You, Night! You're dark because you don't know him.

Daylight! Go find out what it means to shine.

هر جا به جهان تخم وفامی کارد
وان تخم زخرمنگه مامی آرد

هر جا ز طرب نای و دفی بردارد
آن شادی ماست، آن خود پندارد

The Seeds

Each spot on earth where seeds of love are sown,
those seeds have blown to there from my own barn.
Any place where flute and drum are playing,
that's my delight the others think they own.

گه باده لقب نهادم، و گه جامش
گاهی زر پخته، گاه سیم خامش

گه دانه، و گاه صید، و گاهی دامش
این جمله چراست؟ تا نگویم نامش

What's His Name?

I called him *wine*—then said *cup* was his name.

He's raw silver—or gold polished in flame.

He's the seed—the prey—perhaps, the trap!

Why all these questions? I won't say his name.

رفتم به در خانهٔ آن خوش پیوند
بیرون آمد به نزد من خندان چند

اندر بر خود کشیدمش چون قند
کای عاشق وای عارف وای دانشمند

Unity

I went to the house of his unity.
He came out of the door and laughed at me.
Sweet as sugar, he took me in his arms,
said: "My Lover! My Scholar! My Sufi!"

در عشق تو ام نصیحت و پند چه سود؟
زهراب چشیده ام مرا قند چه سود؟

گویند مرا که: «بند بر پایش نهید»
دیوانه دلست، پام بر، بند چه سود؟

Tie His Feet!

I'm in love. So, reason? What good is that?
I took poison. Sugar? What good is that?
They yell: Go tie his feet! But it's my heart
that's crazy. Tie my feet? What good is that?

نامهربان نگار، با وفایم نگرفت
پس بودم، او چو کیمیایم نگرفت

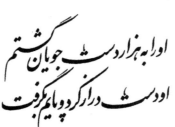

او را به هزار دست جویان گشتم
او دست درآر کرد و پایم نگرفت

He Grabbed Me

My lover looked, his glance of love caught hold.

Like magic, I was copper turned to gold.

I tried to touch him, tried a thousand ways.

At last, he grabbed my leg and kept ahold.

من عاشق عشق و عشق هم عاشق من
تن عاشق جان آمد و جان عاشق تن

گه من آرم دو دست در گردن او
گه او کشدم چو دلبر پایان گردن

I Am in Love

I am in love with love, and Love with me.

My body lusts for soul, and Soul for me.

Sometimes, I put both arms around his neck.

Sometimes, he sighs and brings his face to me.

در انجمنی نشسته دیدم، دوشش
نتوانستم گرفت در آغوشش

رخ را به بهانه بر رخش بنهادم
یعنی که حدیث می‌کنم در گوشش

Holy Words

Last night, I saw him sit with others here.
I couldn't take him in my arms for fear
of them. So, I brought my face to his—faked
some holy words to whisper in his ear.

سر در سر خاک آستان تو نهم
دل در خم زلف دلستان تو نهم

جانم به لب آمده است، لب پیش من آر
تا جان به بهانه در دهان تو نهم

One Kiss

My head sits on your doorstep over there—
I threw my heart into your tangled hair.
My soul is on these lips. Bring your lips close!
For one kiss you can have my soul, I swear.

صد روز دراز ازگر بھم پویدی
جان را نشود ازین فغان خرسندی

ای آنک بدین حدیث ما می خندی
مجنون نشدی هنوز دانشمندی

Longing

I lie with my lover a hundred days,
and still my heart cannot end its longing.
Hey! You may laugh at that. But you're still
an intellectual. Wait till you go mad!

دیوانه شدم خواب ز دیوانه خطاست
دیوانه چه داند که ره خواب کجاست

زیرا که خدا نخفت و پاکست ز خواب
مجنون خدا بدان هم از خواب جداست

Madness

I have gone mad, and madmen never sleep.
A madman, what does he know about sleep?
You know: God doesn't sleep. So, none of that!
You know: I'm mad with Love, so I can't sleep.

در عشق که جز می بقا خوردن نیست
جز جان دادن دلیل جان دادن نیست

گفتم که تو را شناسم آنگه بپرم
گفتا که شناسای مرا مردن نیست

Eternal Wine

This wine of love is all there is for me.

Why am I here, if my soul can't be free?

I said: I will know you, then I will die.

He said: "You cannot die, if you know me."

اندر دل من درون و بیرون همه اوست
اندر تن من جان و رگ و خون همه اوست

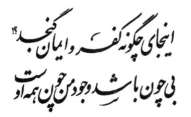

اینجای چگونه کفر و ایمان گنجد
بی چون باشد وجود من چون همه اوست

He Is My Heart

He is my heart, inside and outside, whole.
He is my blood, my veins, my flesh, my soul.
How can faith and no-faith both live inside
me? He is! That's all!—That's my life he stole.

از آتش سودا پی توام تابی بود
در جوی دل از صحبت تو آبی بود

آن آب سراب بود و آن آتش رب
بگذشت کنون قصه مگر خوابی بود

Passion

I burned in fire—that passion for you.
Streams cooled my heart—when together with you.
That water is vapor, that fire now snow.
The story's over. Was love just a dream?

دلدارچو دید خسته و غمگینم
آمد، خندان نشست بر بالینم

خارید سرم، بگفت کای مسکینم
هم می‌نهد دل که چنینت بینم

In Bed

My lover came in. I was sad, in bed.
He smiled at me, and then he scratched my head.
He sat beside me there. "Poor thing! Poor thing!
It hurts my heart to see you so," he said.

گفتم: صنمی شدی، که جان اوطنی
گفتا که: حدیث جان مکن، گر زمنی

گفتم که: به تیغ هجر تم چند زنی
گفتا که: هنوز عاشق خویشتنی

My Love

I said: You are my love, my soul's country!
He said: "Don't talk about your soul if you
love me." I said: You've cut my throat with words!
He said: "You're still in love with self, I see."

اندر دلِ بی‌وفا غم و ماتم باد
آن را که وفا نیست ز عالم کم باد

دیدی که مرا هیچ کسی یاد نکرد؟
جز غم؟ که هزار آفرین بر غم باد

Unfaithful

Fill my faithless heart with grief, with sorrow.
Unfaithful, let me pass out from this world.
See! No one remembered me—but sorrow.
So, a thousand praises to that sorrow!

در عشق اگر دمی قرارت باشد
اندر صف عاشقان چه کارت باشد

ستیز چو چار باش تا یار چو گل
گه در بروگاه برکنارت باشد

You're the Thorn

But in his love, if you are not forlorn—
how can you say you're one of us, his love-torn
lovers? He is the rose. Yes!—in your reach,
by your side!—but, you must become the thorn.

گفتم چشمم گفت براهش میدار
گفتم جگرم گفت پرآبش میدار

گفتم که دلم گفت حه داری در دل
گفتم غم تو گفت نگاهش میدار

So, Keep It!

I said: My eyes? "Stare at the path," he said.

I said: My guts? "Go tear them out," he said.

I said: My heart? He said: "What's in your heart?"

I said: Your sorrow. "So, keep it!" he said.

گفتم : «بنما که چون کنم» گفت : «بمیر»

گفتم که : «شد آب روغنم» گفت : «بمیر»

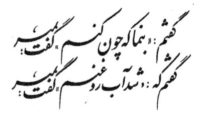

گفتم که : «شوم شمع من پروانه

ای روی تو شمع روشنم» گفت : «بمیر»

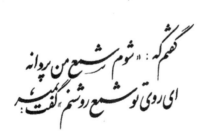

74

Die!

I said: Tell me what to do. He said: "Die!"
I said: But I'm melting down. He said: "Die!"
I said: I'll be a moth to your candle—
your face my burning flame. He said: "Just die!"

خواهم که دلم با غم همخو باشد
گر دست دهد غمش چه نیکو باشد

هان ای دل بی‌دل غم او در گیر
تا چشم زنی خود غم او با او باشد

Sorrow

I wish my heart could accept this sorrow,
could even feel perfect joy in sorrow.
My cold, my empty heart! Why can't you see?
He himself is sorrow. Find that sorrow!

این سینه پر مشغله از مکتب اوست
وامروز که بیمار شدم از تب اوست

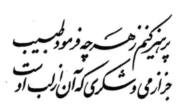

پرهیز کنم زهر چه فرمود طبیب
جز از می و شکری که آن از لب اوست

Bring Wine!

This burning heart is the cost of his school;
and today, my high fever is his cruel
lesson. Bring wine! No medicine. I'll take
wine—cool wine, and the sugar on his lips.

دل برد ز من دوش، بصد عشق فسون
بشکافت و بدید، پر زخون بود درون

فرمود، در آتش نهادن خالی
یعنی که نپخته‌ست، از آتش پرخون

Bleeding

Last night, with all his charm, he stole my heart.
It bled a lot when he tore it apart.
He said: "Put him back in fire. He's raw.
Uncooked! That's why he has a bleeding heart."

در بادیهٔ عشق تو کردم سفری
تا بو که بیابم ز وصالت خبری

در هر منزل که می نهادم قدمی
افکنده تنی دیدم و افتاده سری

The Corpses

The desert of your love I traveled through,
to try to find some way to be with you.
From house to house, I saw just severed heads
you left behind, and corpses that you slew.

از عشق تو آتش جوا سپنے خیزد؛
در سینه حمالهای جانے خیزد

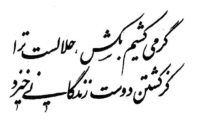

گرمی کشیم بکش، حلالست ترا
گر کشتن دوست زندگانے خیزد

Fire and Love

From fire and love something new will rise,
and inside my heart, a new life will rise.
If you want to kill me—do it! That's good!
When my Friend kills me, then I'll surely rise.

هر روز دلم در غم تو زارتر است
وز من دل بی رحم تو بیزارتر است

بگذاشتیم غم تو نگذاشت مرا
حقا که غمت از تو وفادارتر است

Cruel Heart

Each day my heart, it finds more grief in you.
And your cruel heart is tired of it, too.
Now you've left me. But your sorrow's still here.
Your sorrow! It's more true to me than you.

دوشینه مرا گذاشتی خوش خفتی
واشب به دل به هر سویی می رفتی

گفتم که: مرا تا به قیامت خفتی
کو آن سخنی که وقت مستی گفتی

Your Drunken Vows

Last night, you left—had a good sleep out there.
Tonight, you're gone, fooling around somewhere.
I thought you'd lie next to me forever—
So, where are all the drunken vows you swear?

دوش آمد یار بر در، دم شیدایی
گفتم که: برو که امشب المدمایی

می‌رفت و همی‌گفت: زهی سودایی
دولت به درآمدست، در نگشایی

Go Away!

Last night—he was trembling—my lover came
to stay. I said: Tonight, no! Go away!
He left and said: "What faith! What faith! Fortune
came to your door, and you sent me away."

گر صبر کنی پرده صبرت بدریم
ور خواب روی ز خواب رختت ببریم

گر کوه شوی در آتشت بگذاریم
ور بحر شوی تمام آبت بخوریم

If You . . .

Be patient—and I'll tear your patience up!
Sleep. Then, I'll rip the sleep from your eyecup.
Be a mountain. I'll set you on fire.
If you become the sea, I'll drink you up!

خوش خوش صنما، تازه رُخان آمده
خندان، بدولب لعل گُزان آمده

آن روز دلم ز سینه بُدی بس نیست
کامروز دگر به قصد جان آمده

Good, Good!

Good, good! My lover's come with a new face,
and laughing this time, with lips ruby red!
Not enough you've torn my heart from its place . . .
No! Now you're back, and now you want me dead.

خواهم که گردی که از هوای تو رسد
باشد که بدیده خاک پای تو رسد

جانم زجفا خرّم و خندان باشد
زیرا زجفا بوی وفای تو رسد

Only Dust

To touch the dust that rises from your feet!
To see it even, that is just as sweet!
My life of pain, it is filled up with joy!
Your cruelty only makes my faith complete.

تا در دل من عشق تو افسرده شد
جز عشق تو هر چه داشتم شُسته شد

عقل و سبق و کتاب بر طاق نهاد
شعر و غزل و دوبیتی آموخته شد

Love Songs

When in my heart your love set up its fire,
it burned up all I had except desire.
I put away my reason, books, and pride.
I sang love songs—and rhymes became my guide.

ما کار و دکان و پیشه را سوخته‌ایم
شعر و غزل و دو بیتی آموخته‌ایم

در عشق، که او جان و دل و دیده ماست
جان و دل و دیده، هر سه را سوخته‌ایم

My Calling

My work, my shop, my tools—I burned them all.
Then poems, songs, and rhymes were my life's call.
In love—I found my heart, my soul, my hope.
Then, heart and soul and hope—I burned them all.

دستارم و جبه و پسرم، هر سه بهم
قیمت کردند، به یک درم چیزی کم

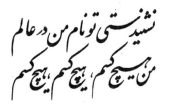

نشنیدستی تو نام من در عالم
من هیچ کسم، هیچ کسم، هیچ کسم

I'm Nobody

My cloak, my turban, and my head—all three:
Together they are not worth a penny.
Haven't you heard my name, known 'round the world?
I'm nobody. Nobody! Nobody!

هم کُهنم و هم دینم و هم صافم و دُرد
هم پیرم و هم جوان و هم کودک خُرد

گر من بمِرَم مرا مگویید که: مُرد
گو: مرده بُد و زنده شد و دوست ببُرد

Don't Say I Died

Evil and good—pure wine and dregs—am I.
Now old—now young—a newborn babe am I!
When I die, don't say that he died. Just say:
His lover woke him up, took him away.

دو کون خیال خانه‌ای بیش نبود
وامد ما بهانه‌ای بیش نبود

عمری‌ست که قصه‌ای زجان می‌شنوی
قصه حکنم فسانه‌ای بیش نبود

No More

Two worlds I dreamed . . . were just a house—no more.

My comings and goings were an excuse—

no more. This lifelong story you have heard . . .

What can I say? It's just a tale—no more.

Rumi the Poet

Amin Banani

The history of Muslim mystics includes many profound thinkers, innumerable memorable poets, and quite a few commentators who expressed their thought in verse. Without a doubt, none has attained the heights of mystic insight and experience, or the poetic expression, reached by Rumi. This bold claim easily extends across all the major tongues of the Muslim world—Arabic, Persian, Turkish, and Urdu—and covers the span of time from the birth of Islam to the present. Yet the overwhelming amount of attention paid to him, whether by scholarly observers or devotees, by those who have learned his language or are native speakers of it, has been to the system and content of his thought.

Considerations of Rumi the poet are often subordinated to the discussion of his doctrinal and philosophical views. This imbalance is aggravated by a number of factors. First is Rumi's frequent fulminations against the concerns and the craft of poets and his disclaimers of his own interest in his poetry. Then there are the myths surrounding his poetic practice. And finally, there are his frequent judgments, albeit made with an air of embarrassment, regarding his "shortcomings" as a poet.

An earlier version of this essay was published in *Poetry and Mysticism in Islam: The Heritage of Rumi*, Amin Banani, Richard Hovannisian, and Georges Sabagh, eds. (Cambridge University Press, 1994), pp. 28-43.

In the confusion and contradiction the above reasons create, much is implied but little is made clear about the Persian poetic tradition and the prevailing native theory of poetry during Rumi's time. This study is a token beginning toward a reexamination which, it is hoped, may lead to a redefinition, for devotees and students of Persian poetry, of what poetry is and where Rumi stands in relation to it.

The title of this short essay may also suggest that it is possible to focus upon only one dimension of the complex but wholly integrated person that was Rumi. Nothing could be farther from the truth. The source and the structure of his mystical thought and the nature and process of his poetic creativity are inseparably connected. It is, in fact, in the nexus of the two that the core of the man is to be sought.

The Confluence of Opposites

The tension between mystical and legalistic tendencies—present in all Abrahamic religious traditions—is nowhere more pronounced than in Islam. Mysticism as a variety of religious experience in Islamic history has commonly come to be known as Sufism. The figure of Mawlana Jalal al-Din Balkhi (1207-1273), known as Rumi, towers above the mystics of Islam as a Sufi master whose life and works are the validation of a unique paradox. He was at once an ecstatically uninhibited lover of the Divine and a zealous upholder of Islamic Law. It is not merely the profundity of his exposition of the mystic worldview that distinguishes him among a vast and brilliant constellation of Sufi masters, but the volcanic creativity of infinite imagination, the prodigious complexity of his personality and his encounter with life and society of his time—at once sublimely detached and passionately involved.

A man who gave refuge to the homeless, and whose company was sought by royalty. A magnetic force in the process of Islamization in Asia Minor, and yet a man who was deeply loved and, at his death, sincerely mourned by Jews, Greeks, and Armenians alike. A sober judge and expounder of the Holy Law and Doctrine who instituted nocturnal séances of dance and music among his devotees. A man of acute aesthetic sensitivity who even designed the distinctive flowing robe and tall headgear of his circles of dervishes. A supreme creator and manipulator of sign and symbol in an integrated life of infinite variety and singular purpose. This is the legacy left to us by Rumi.

No part of this legacy is more relevant to our time than Rumi's frequent assertions that all religions and revelations are only the rays of a single Sun of Reality, that all prophets have only delivered— albeit in different tongues—the same principles of eternal goodness and eternal truth. The ultimate goal of humanity, according to Rumi, is union with God through love. Virtue, as he conceives it, is not an end but a means to that end. Thus his poetry is based on a transcendental idea of unity which he works out from the moral, not the metaphysical, standpoint. It is the primacy and the power of love as the animating motive of that moral view that gives Rumi's Sufism an ultimately affirmative view of the human predicament.

As modern human beings experience, with growing bitterness and deepening anguish, the fragmentation of our own beings and our alienation from all that surrounds us, the seeming wholeness of another era beckons to us with increasing allure. Still, as Rumi warns, the line between self-knowledge and self-delusion is thin and elusive. Rumi strove to "annihilate" his "self" in search of the Beloved. Others rather have sought to assert theirs, in that same quest. Some have traveled a circular path to selflessness and arrived at self-indulgence.

It was their focus on the primary place of the spiritual dimension in human experience which enabled the Sufis to overcome their sense of separation with exuberant joy. The possibility of recapturing our spiritual potential reenters into the vision of our time, and it depends upon awareness of ourselves.

The Persian Poetic Tradition

Few cultural traditions are as permeated with poetry as that of the Persian-speaking world. By the same token, there are not many people whose critical judgment about the nature and quality of poetry is as dulled by the sheer quantity of verse that has been compiled over a millennium of literary tradition. Even before the accumulation of this massive body of formal verse, circumstances pertaining to the cultural milieu in which the tradition was nurtured—the taste of its intended audience, the social position and function of the poet, the nature of patronage, and above all, the character of its overweening model—had much to do with defining the aesthetic principles which have guided poets writing in the Persian language and governed the judgment of their labors.

However much we might conjecture about the presence of lively poetic veins among the lower strata of Perso-Islamic societies—and there is ample evidence for such conjecture in the preserved snatches of topical verse and street ballads—there is no denying that the chronicles of Persian poetic history and the canons of Persian poetic taste were conceived and formulated in princely courts and ruling circles, beginning in the ninth century in eastern Iran and spreading to other regions of the Persephone world. In this milieu, we recognize an earlier bardic tradition whose primary function was entertainment. The bards provided song and music for the royal *bazm*, the ceremonial banquet. They would sing lyrics of their own composition and accompany themselves on a musical instrument. The roots of this tradition can be found in pre-Islamic Iran. Typified by Kudaki, they show a preference for the *masnavi* genre for their longer idylls, the shorter *tarane* for wine and nature poems, and *ghazal* for love poetry. The common wisdom has identified the ghazal as the "detached head" of the Arabic *qasida*. Only the relatively recent investigations by Alessandro Bausani suggest a possible earlier pre-Islamic provenance for the ghazal by pointing to a Chinese poetic form allegedly modeled after lyrics brought to China by Persian court musicians.[1] The Chinese poems are remarkable in their formal resemblance to the ghazal, including the recognizable rhyme scheme.

The bardic tradition was soon merged with a class of patronized panegyrists whose function was essentially political. They spun a mantle of virtue and legitimacy for patrons who often lacked both. In their role and social position, they resemble more the tribal poets of pre-Islamic Arabia and the panegyrists of the Umayyad and the Abbasid courts. Their preferred mode of expression was the qasida, modeled after the classical Arabic genre. By the time this class of professional court poets of the Persian language assumed their principal role as panegyrists, the aesthetic principles governing their activities and the canons of taste applied to their words were firmly established in the Arabic model. Poetry was defined simply as metered and rhymed speech. Its practitioners viewed themselves as craftsmen, builders whose brick and mortar consisted of an established supply of rhetorical devices. The novel and ingenious employment of these devices was pursued as an end in itself. The success of a "construction" was measured in discrete and segmented parts of the whole. The intention of the poet was to evoke a sense of marvel and amazement in his audience by the brilliance of those formal parts. The themes were known and prescribed and could not be expected to surprise or fascinate.

Within the given cultural context, and adhering to the poetic principles described above, much poetry of exquisite artistry was written in Arabic and Persian. The stamp of poetic tradition was configured in this milieu, and it has continued to dominate the standards of poetic taste to this date.[2] But princely courts did not remain the exclusive source of the patronage, production, and consumption of Persian poetry. Once more, from the eastern regions of the Persian world, this time from the Sufi circles, the voice of poetry was raised. It was Sana'i, a court poet of Ghazna, who made a decisive transformation in his own life and, as it turned out, a signal turn in the course of Persian poetry. He employed the molds and forms, the tools and devices, developed by the bards and the panegyrists for a new and different purpose: the affirmation of a mystical worldview.

If the hybrid verse of Sana'i pointed the way, it was the fired imagination of 'Attar that transmitted mystical thought into pure art and limned the sea of soul into which Rumi so boldly stepped.

The Ghazal as a Mystic Form

Whereas Sana'i and 'Attar had chosen the narrative masnavi as the primary vehicle of their mystic verse, Rumi began with the ghazal form and undoubtedly stayed with it to the end of his life, turning only later to the masnavi, which also occupied him to the end. The ghazal is the quintessential Persian poetic form, certainly the most popular and the most enduring. By virtue of its ubiquity, it is at once the most noble and most debased genre to be encountered in Persian poetry. It achieved its zenith of perfection in the period extending from the thirteenth to the fourteenth centuries, when poets of such immense power as Sa'di, Rumi, and Hafez poured their creativity into it.

It is no mere coincidence that this high period of the Persian ghazal is also the time when it was the preferred vehicle for expressing the mystical aspirations of the soul. Of the three supreme practitioners of the art, it was Rumi who fused the mystic vocabulary and the language of the ghazal, the predominant ethos of mysticism as well as the intricate fabric of symbolism, to such an extent that ghazal as a form took on a unitary vision of the universe. It could be argued, for example, that it was Rumi's conflating of the purest mystical spirit with the most corporeal sensuality that paved the way for Hafez's tantalizing irony and ambivalence. This inherent affinity between the ghazal form and the mystic vision cannot be overemphasized. What seems to be a bewildering variety of images and ideas in a ghazal is fused together into a unity by the Sufi poet, much in the same way as the mystic reduces the diversity and the multiplicity of the phenomenal universe into one world of divine spirit. Those who have puzzled over the incoherence of the imagery and the apparent absence of structural unity in the ghazal have been looking for a rational scheme of organization, an intellectual coherence, a logical progression, a dramatic continuity—in short, for reason. Reason is precisely what Rumi considers a shackle. For him, the animating force of existence is love, equated with *unreason*. No concept has been more vigorously attacked and subjected to more withering ridicule by Rumi than reason. The greatest portion of his lyrical poetry, that is, his ghazals, is a rhapsodic celebration of love, which, as he emphatically tells us, is a force diametrically opposed to reason.

Here lies the nexus of Rumi the mystic and Rumi the poet, and it is at this point that we must make sense of the mythified accounts of how Rumi came to be a poet. The poetry that welled up in him and continued to explode like volcanic eruptions was precisely that stream of irrational and enraptured, love-crazed, magical incantations described and disapproved by Plato. The list of uneven and doomed contests between reason and love that one encounters in Rumi's poetry is endless. Love (*'eshq*) is often represented in a metonymic way by one of its attributes, such as drunkenness (*masti*), madness (*divanegi, junun*), or unconsciousness (*bikhodi*).

The link with madness is particularly potent with poetic possibilities, because it makes possible a play on the concrete root of its opposite, *aql* (wisdom, reason—also, the camel's knee-lock). It is the shackle that ties down the camel, particularly the *shotor-e mast*, the drunken camel (that is, the rutting camel), to prevent it from wandering off into the desert, just as Majnun, the love-crazed legendary lover, wandered off into the wilderness. With the figure of

Majnun, the semantic domains of love and madness are joined into one in Sufi symbolism, and wine and drunkenness become the symbols of the unhobbled spirit, the best way to remove the shackle of reason.

This is but a glimpse at the substance of Rumi's poetry. To search it for a scheme of rational organization and discursive language is to deny the very source of its vision. The brilliance and heterogeneity of his imagery point toward a transcendence of speech itself. The character of his best ghazals is that of music rising above words and letters and transcending the murmur of syllables and sounds, freed from the bonds of rational discourse but obeying a higher harmony.

> *Ta chand ghazalhara dar surat-e harf ari*
> *Bi surat-e harf az jan beshno ghazali digar* [3]

How long are you going to put ghazals in the form of speech?

Without speech, hear another ghazal from the soul.

It is precisely in this faithful reflection of the paradox of our existence—order in chaos, unity in multiplicity, songs without words—that Rumi discovers his art.

Rumi's Art

Let us hear it in his own language and marvel at how much he reveals in so few words:

> *Shams-e Tabrizi be ruham chang zad*
> *Lajeram dar 'eshq gashtam arghanun.* [4]

The line is constructed on a pun and therefore de-
fies simple translation. One might give its surface
sense by simply saying:

> Shams-e Tabrizi touched my soul.
> Then (inevitably), I became an organ on
>   (the subject of) love

But "touched" misses the crux of the matter.
The wordplay is on the double meaning of the
compound verb *chang zadan*, made up of the noun
chang and the verb *zadan*. The noun *chang* means
paw, claw, talon; and with the auxiliary verb *zadan*,
to strike, it becomes: to claw, to dig one's fingers
into (something). There is a definite connotation of
forcefulness and violence. The preposition *be* before
ruham (my soul) grammatically reinforces this
sense of the verb. So the initial image projected is:
"Shams-e Tabrizi reached into my soul," or better,
"dug his fingers into my soul." But the mention of
arghanun—a musical instrument—as the last word
of the poem immediately brings up the second
meaning of *chang* as a harp or lyre, and undoubtedly
so named because of its resemblance to a digitated
paw or hand, and because it is played by the pluck-
ing of the stretched fingers. The auxiliary verb
zadan is the usual one in Persian for playing any
musical instrument. So the second image evoked is
that "Shams-e Tabrizi played the lyre *with* my soul."
Once more it is the preposition *be* that carries the
weight of subtlety. It is the very soul of Rumi that
is the lyre, and it is the fingers of Shams that reach

in and play upon it. The two images projected by the two meanings of *chang zadan* are superimposed, and precisely in a *musical* way, the tension created by the violence of the first meaning is released by the caressing harmony of the second.

The sense of conjoining opposites—a reflection of the essential paradox—is intensified in the second line. "Inevitably in love" (*dar 'eshq*), used here in the abstract verbal noun form, casting its semantic net across the entire range of love: "I became an *arghanun*." Why the choice of *arghanun*, a musical instrument seldom mentioned in connection with the Sufis? Why not the ubiquitous *nay* or *barbat* or *daff*? Because, unlike all those instruments, which require the active fingering and fretting of the player in order to produce the desired tones, the *arghanun* is pre-tuned. Thus an involuntary musical order is already built into it. It serves as an apt metaphor for the spontaneity, as well as the ultimate harmony, of Rumi's poetry—but it is an ordered harmony on the subject of love, which is equated with madness.

Here we may look for the grounds of what Western scholars of Arabic and Persian literature have often objected to as the bewildering heterogeneity of images in the ghazal. For this feature in ghazal is in fact a closely related aspect of the non-discursive thought process. Both features are deeply rooted within the underlying mystic vision and override the discursive regimentation of thought at a deeper organizational level, the level of imagery. They dispose with most of those tangible linkages between images which our discursive habit of mind requires in order to cross from one to the other; for the heavier the referential and logical freight of thought, the more solid the connecting bridges must be. The disembodied, ethereal substance of Sufi thought rarely stands in need of such stepping stones. Moreover, the objects of experience which would, in the factual regard, appear to be in fragments and disjointed would, in the light of the mystic vision, merge and blend in an all-encompassing unity of being.

Transcending Words

In hardly any other poetry is the fluid coalescence of heterogeneous images achieved more wondrously than in the poems of Rumi. They overwhelm by a deluge of imagery, the heterogeneity of which is miraculously subdued into unity, in the light of a frightening clairvoyance. One particular verse singularly illustrates both the unifying-subduing process of Rumi's style and the penetrating force of his visionary poetry:[5]

> *Cho dig az zar bovad u ra siyah-rui'i che gham arad*
> *Ke'az janash hami tabad be har zakhmi hekayatha* [6]

> Being of gold, why should the pot grieve at
>   a blackened face?
> For through each gash, emanate dazzling
>   tales of its soul.

In this verse, Rumi compacts a brilliant allegory of the body-soul dichotomy. He proceeds by systematically chipping away, as it were, the blackened crust of matter in which the treasure of the spirit has been trapped, until the very golden heart shines forth. He does this at several stages of successive penetration. First, by giving a face to the pot, he animates it. Then he humanizes it by suggesting its grief at the disgrace of falling into the toilsome prison of dark matter—the play on the double meaning of "black face," that is, the darkened exterior "face" of the pot as well as disgrace and infamy, is true to the grain. Yet even the tragic identity of the toiling, begrimed, but nobly wrought being does not end with the process of removing the multiple layers of appearances from the face of the inner reality. There remains one more crucial veil which, once unfolded, will reveal the humanized being as deified. The chipping process at this point scores "gashes" (*zakhm*) upon the darkened body, revealing the pure gold of the soul. The metaphor reverberates with allusions to the wounds of the prophets and the anguished bodies of the saints—the luminous gold which radiates through the gashes, symbolizing the efflux of their sanctified blood.

Here the style passes into a still higher level of spirituality. The tales of the unveiled soul "emanate" (*hami tabad*), that is to say, they are not conveyed verbally, but shine forth from the inner reality of being, once the black veil of matter has been rent through.

This striking metaphor distills—to the extent that a single metaphor may be capable of distilling—Rumi's idea of the function, or rather the ambition, of poetry, which for him is telling the story of the soul by means which transcend the range of words.

The inadequacy of words, the hopeless venture of "crippled" logic and blind intellect in the mystic quest, are all varying aspects of a pervasive theme in Rumi's poetry, which aspires to transcend words through words. This inveterate concern is voiced right at the beginning of the Masnavi:

> *Gar che tafsir-e zaban rowshangar ast*
> *Lik 'eshq-e bi zaban rowshantar ast*
> *Chun qalam andar neveshtan mishetaft*
> *Chun be 'eshq amad qalam az ham shekaft* [7]

> Illuminating as is the account of words,
> Yet more lucid the tongue of wordless love.
> As the pen was racing along its path,
> It split through as it came upon love.

The foregoing discussion is only a passing glance at Rumi's attitude toward discursive language and at his manner of gorging a verbal medium, out of his poetry, toward achieving a transverbal "telling." It is no coincidence that Rumi alludes particularly to this function of his poetry in the very first line of the Masnavi, where he evokes the sublime symbol of the reed, whose melody shapes not only the opening line but epitomizes the ideal end of his poetry. This view of Rumi's poetry as an immediate emanation of the aspiring and rapt soul, rather than a mediate structure of a discursive scheme, is further affirmed by his unconventional manner of composing. For, if we are to believe the stories, he never betook himself to pen and paper in order to write a ghazal. His poems were spontaneous effusions of mystical ecstasy, recorded by his disciples. How far we are from the verbal gymnastics of the professional poets and their shoddy imitators! How perfect even the form can be when the poet starts out with something worth saying. Not until the middle of the twentieth century, and then only in response to different circumstances, was the fixation on the formal definition of poetry challenged in Persian culture. Therein lies a vital link between Rumi and our own outlook and experience. In rejecting the primacy of form, Rumi placed himself outside the mainstream of Persian poetic tradition. It may be time to redefine and reappraise that tradition, with Rumi at the center of it.

ENDNOTES

1. Alessandro Bausani, "La Persia nel Medievo," *Annali della Academia Nazionale dei Lincei* (Rome, 1971).
2. Shams-e Qays Razi, *Al-Moj'am* (Tehran, 1957).
3. Rumi, *Divan-e Shams*, ed. By B. Foruzanfar (Tehran: 1964), p. 409. Except where otherwise noted, all translations are mine.
4. Ali Dashti, *Seyri dar Divan-e Shams* (Tehran, 1958), p. 8.
5. For some of the illustrations, I am indebted to Hedayat Izadpanah, whose analysis of Persian lyric poetry is unmatched in the field.
6. Rumi, *Divan*, p. 72.
7. Rumi, *Masnavi* (Tehran, 1964), p. 128.

Bibliography

The poems in this book can be found in two collections of Rumi's works:

Bahiuzzaman Furuzanfar, ed. *Kulliyat-e Shams-e Tabrizi.* Tehran: Amir Kabir Press, 12ᵗʰ Edition, 1988.

————, ed. *Kulliyat-e Shams.* Tehran: University of Tehran, First Edition, 1963. Volume 8.

The Persian calligraphy was written by Massoud Valipour and has been reproduced with permission from: Shahram T. Shiva. *Rending the Veil: Literal and Poetic Translations of Rumi.* Prescott, AZ: Hohm Press, 1995.

The numbers of the poems found in the source volumes are provided below, followed by AK to indicate the Amir Kabir edition and UT to indicate the University of Tehran edition. This is the same numbering system used in Shiva's volume cited above.

> *Being* 366 UT
> *Bleeding* 1506 UT
> *Bring Wine!* 318 UT
> *Come Here* 2 AK
> *The Corpses* 1854 AK
> *Cruel Heart* 447 AK
> *Die!* 930 UT
> *Don't Come Here* 60 AK
> *Don't Say I Died* 519 UT
> *Don't Think* 936 AK
> *Eternal Wine* 311 AK
> *Fire and Love* 557 UT
> *Go Away!* 1950 UT
> *Good, Good!* 1662 UT
> *Half Moon* 1262 UT
> *He Grabbed Me* 411 UT
> *He Is My Heart* 321 UT
> *Holy Words* 1012 UT